THE BUSINESS PLAN
WRITE-UP SIMPLIFIED

I0491122

THE BUSINESS PLAN WRITE-UP SIMPLIFIED

A PRACTITIONER'S GUIDE TO WRITING THE BUSINESS PLAN

SARADA RAMANI

Notion Press

Old No. 38, New No. 6
McNichols Road, Chetpet
Chennai - 600 031

First Published by Notion Press 2017
Copyright © Sarada Ramani 2017
All Rights Reserved.

ISBN 978-1-946641-21-2

This book has been published with all reasonable efforts taken to make the material error-free after the consent of the author. No part of this book shall be used, reproduced in any manner whatsoever without written permission from the author, except in the case of brief quotations embodied in critical articles and reviews.

The Author of this book is solely responsible and liable for its content including but not limited to the views, representations, descriptions, statements, information, opinions and references ["Content"]. The Content of this book shall not constitute or be construed or deemed to reflect the opinion or expression of the Publisher or Editor. Neither the Publisher nor Editor endorse or approve the Content of this book or guarantee the reliability, accuracy or completeness of the Content published herein and do not make any representations or warranties of any kind, express or implied, including but not limited to the implied warranties of merchantability, fitness for a particular purpose. The Publisher and Editor shall not be liable whatsoever for any errors, omissions, whether such errors or omissions result from negligence, accident, or any other cause or claims for loss or damages of any kind, including without limitation, indirect or consequential loss or damage arising out of use, inability to use, or about the reliability, accuracy or sufficiency of the information contained in this book.

This book is dedicated to

Ramani Ramachandran, my life and business partner who made me
What am I today

And

my lovely daughters Ramya and Sowmya —who have been enabling me
to Take every Step in my own Way.

My sincere thanks to My father late Shri Raman & my mother
Balambal Raman, My mother in law Late Kalpagam and all
my inlaws, co-sisters, my brothers and sisters in law

And

my Advisors and Mentors and all my friends.

A special thanks to Umashree for helping me with the editing.

Contents

CONTENTS

Preface

I am a self-made person. From being stay at home happy mother of two lovely daughters and a great wife to an excellent human being for fourteen long and glorious years, i transformed to a successful Entrepreneur of an IT products and services company based out of Chennai, India and doing business across the globe including North America, South America, Africa, Europe, UK, the Middle East, Singapore, Vietnam, Malaysia, Australia and Japan, and of course, in India. This has been possible because of my husband **Ramani Ramachandran,** advisors and support of family and friends.

During the course of this entrepreneurial journey (that I have been pursuing in my own way with no formal coaching or mentorship,) I realized that if I can achieve this much of success, how much more could I have achieved if only I had the necessary business tools.

Once such tool is the **Business Plan** and even now I am surprised that there are a lot of young entrepreneurs who struggle with it. When I ask them to show me their business plan, they say they will come back by the next week, and they do come back with a document called the Business Plan. What have they done in the interim?

- Went to the most powerful God in the universe – Google
- Searched for 'business plan'
- Got a few templates for free
- Filled it with both relevant and irrelevant data
- Presented it to me.

I have encountered this scenario over and over again, and thus, I came up with the idea of authoring this book on business plan.

I have taken care to make it simple and have used no jargons or no MBA course material. I have also made sure that I am providing different examples for various scenarios. May you benefit by the mistakes of others and become successful in your endeavours!

Introduction

I have always been fascinated with Mount Everest. However, in my age and physical condition, I can only dream about it and cheer those who have climbed or will be climbing the world's highest peak, with its peak measuring 8,848 metres (29,029 ft.) above sea level. The summit is in the border of Nepal to the south, and China or Tibet on the North. It is over 60 million years old. The Everest was formed by the movement of the Indian tectonic plate pushing up and against the Asian plate. The Everest grows by about a quarter of an inch (0.25") every year.

Mt. Everest has two main climbing routes, the South-East ridge from Nepal and the North ridge from Tibet. It has many other less frequently climbed routes as well. Of the two main routes, the South-East ridge is technically easier and is frequently used. It was the route used by Edmund Hillary and Tenzing Norgay in 1953, and the first to be recognised of the fifteen routes to the top by 1996. This was, however, a route that was dictated more by politics than by design as the Chinese border was closed to the

Western world in the 1950s after the People's Republic of China invaded Tibet.

Most attempts are made during May before the summer monsoon season. As the monsoon season approaches, a change in the jet stream at this time pushes it northward, thereby reducing the average wind speeds high on the mountain. Attempts are sometimes made after the monsoons in September and October, when the jet stream is again temporarily pushed northward. But the additional snow deposited by the monsoons and the less stable weather patterns (the tail end of the monsoon) makes climbing extremely difficult.

I can hear the murmur – *But isn't this book about business plan and not about Mount Everest?* "Patience, my dear Watson," as the famous detective says.

Our business journey is also akin to mountaineering. Not all of us can climb Mt Everest, but according to our ability and our business success, it can be referred as a Himalayan task, and thus, we can also successfully claim our right to have been atop the world's highest peak.

Please note that in the above narration, there are several clues to not just writing our business plan, but also for our business success.

1. Getting the measure of the market and understanding it thoroughly.

2. The political climate about the market and the effects of our plan and how to change them according to the situation. Though one strategy is easier, yet we may not be able to adapt it.

3. The timing that needs to be planned.

4. Preparedness, planning, forming the right team and taking the support of people and tools to reach our goals.

Throughout the book, I intend on giving some of the firsts with regard to the reaching of the summit, as I want all readers to be reaching their respective summits despite all the challenges and difficult conditions.

An Entrepreneur

WHAT IS ENTREPRENEURSHIP?

This is a very basic question, but when I wanted to start writing the explanation, I was stumped. Yes, the meaning in the dictionary is simple, but is it so simple? My answer is both yes and no.

In Merriam-Webster's dictionary, an entrepreneur is **"one who organizes, manages and assumes the risks of a business or enterprise."**

It is simple. My flower vendor at the corner of the road or my vegetable vendor with a push cart certify to the simplicity of the meaning, Then if it is so simple, why are many of us struggling? May be it has got to do with the **complexity of the business**? I don't think so, because even many a vegetable vendor have given up and ended up with losses. Over the years, the Forbes 100 list has been changing. Some of the top 100 in the last century are no more there...

I can go on about this topic, but I am parking it here. Let's get on to the traits of an entrepreneur.

The Traits of a Successful Entrepreneur

An entrepreneur is the one who fulfils the need of a person or a company, either with a service or a product. In some cases, he or she is the one who creates the need. For example, Mark Zuckerberg. Prior to him there was no Facebook. We did network, but we did it in small circles. Today the reach is so wide that we can search and find out many lost friends, make new friends (with caution of course) and so on and so forth.

Entrepreneurship is not just about

- a brilliant idea or
- filling the need or
- providing a solution to a problem.

It is much more than that. A brilliant idea may not be a successful business venture. Filling the need can become only a temporary phenomenon, or providing a solution may lead to a different need, and thus, the solution may itself be a problem.

It is also about

- endurance
- perseverance
- rigid doggedness

Apart from

- strategy
- planning
- execution
- research analysis

And a bit of luck as well.

Why a Business Plan?

Will a business succeed with only a business plan?

When I started my business way back in 1996, I didn't even know the spelling of entrepreneur let alone know that there were these two magic words called business plan. Of course, applying for loan, I took the best brain/talent in the world – my husband (who was a banker then) to create a project plan and do the cash flow. If I had to present it to an investor, I don't think they would have given me any money as I wouldn't have understood anything on it. (Even today, I have a weakness when it comes to reading through numbers. I can quickly read pages and pages of written text, but give me numbers and I would become reading impaired!!!!) Later on, it was fine-tuned by my auditor when we were actually getting the manna from heaven – the cheque for the loan amount to be deposited in my bank or the pay order for my vendors who were eagerly waiting for its arrival. So I succeeded without a business plan, didn't I?

Right and wrong. I did succeed, but I would have succeeded more if there was this blueprint before me which I now realize in hindsight. But be aware that for a determined entrepreneur, business plan or no business plan – it is business as usual!

Then what purpose does this term 'Business Plan' serve for an entrepreneur?

    a.   Is it only for the start-ups who faithfully write it at least for the investor community?

    b.   Is it for all?

    c.   At what part of the business should we start to write the business plan?

    d.   When can we get away from writing a business plan?

Purpose

There is no single one purpose, and the saying that "one size doesn't fit all" is very true here too. There are multiple purposes for the business plan document since the intended audience for the business plan are different and the purpose changes with each target audience. In practice, it is the millennial in the digital world who talk loudly about their baby – the start-up – and have their business plan out in the open and ready to be flaunted. Most of the start-ups have a great business plan since it is demanded by the people whom you are approaching for funding. The established corporates have the business plans from each of their units, which when consolidated, become the grand plan of the corporate. Between these two are those that fall through the gaps.

Different Types of Business Plans

1. A high level or a brief plan is written when you are working on an idea. This is to put on paper your thoughts and to make sure that it is raising an interest in the reader as this is mostly used as a tool for evoking the interest of the seed funder for the business opportunity that is being presented. It can also be called the first cut or the teaser for your business. Of course, this will be a brief document explaining on the business opportunity or the idea.

2. The detailed document is the blueprint for your business. Take this opportunity to write out a detailed document which will help you translate your dream or your idea or your baby into a black and white working model. This is the base. From here, based on the purpose, you can roll out or edit or work on some section in detail and present it to the relevant people accordingly.

3. The next purpose is to raise funds either as debt or as equity investment. Both require the business plan or a project report or whatever it is called. You need to give the growth numbers and the profitability story of your business as you are dealing with financiers.

4. Team set up – Whether it is the founding team where you are looking out for potential founders to join you in your entrepreneurial journey or recruiting the dream team - you need to talk about the product offering, its growth potential, etc. Basically, it has to appeal to the audience's appetite for their personal growth.

5. Even in an established concern, you still need the business plan from each business unit to keep on re-establishing the business purpose of the unit which will be outlining the short term/long term goals, the strategy and the plan to achieve the goals.

TOC of a Business Plan

The table of contents is the curtain raiser for any book/ report – it lets the reader knows what they can find in the next few pages. Also, it gives the outline of the entire story. If you notice, it is no different from what the table of contents of this book is all about.

1.	Executive Summary
2.	Introduction
3.	The Problem Statement
4.	The Solution that is on Offer
5.	The market place and the product positioning
6.	Competitor Analysis
7.	The Team
8.	Marketing Strategy

9.	Sales Strategy
10.	Operations Plan
11.	Financial Plan
12.	Milestones
13.	Exit Plan

The above thirteen are essential items. However, based on what the product is about, there may extra points like bibliography or other parameter studies that had happened. For example, if you are going to promote a marketing layout and if you are looking at the investor, you want to add any government notifications that will have a bearing on the increased value of the land holding.

The first summit was on May 29, 1953 by Sir Edmund Hillary from New Zealand and Tenzing Norgay, a Sherpa from Nepal. They climbed from the south side on a British expedition lead by Colonel John Hunt.

The first north side summit was on May 25, 1960 by Nawang Gombu (Tibetan) and Chinese climbers Chu Yin-Hau and Wang Fu-zhou

Executive Summary

As the name indicates, this is the elevator pitch to the concept, execution, funding, financials etc. Look for a one page write-up which will focus on the problem statement, on how your product is the right fit, on how customers can get your solution, on the costs involved in developing it, selling it and selling it again. Last but not the least, on what profits you can generate and when. Remember... all these in one single page.

5.2 INTRODUCTION

It is the place holder for the entire story to unfold – how you came to know the problem, or how you perceived the demand etc. are told here. You can start with the helicopter view and talk in generalities.

Example: A person crash-landed into an African village and found that nobody was wearing shoes. There were a lot of people who were limping because they walked on thorns or because the pathway was littered with small stones which cut into their feet. This person found an ideal situation of setting up a shoe factory to manufacture and sell the natives the new product called 'Manna from Heaven' by giving free samples to the school children and to a few elders and by making them wear it for few days and making them narrate their experience of 'no blisters' story to others.

The first woman to summit Everest was Junko Tabei of Japan in 1975. 1975 is also marked by first female ascent from the North Ridge, by Phanthog, deputy head of the second Chinese Everest expedition that sent nine climbers to the summit.

The Problem Statement

This is the plot of an Agatha Christy novel. The entire bulk of your business, let alone your business plan, rests on this plot. How you are able to clearly write about the problem statement will help you, the business owner, to get the best solution.

This section will talk about

    a.   What the current situation is.

    b.   How the problem affects customers or how customers are suffering with the current situation.

Let's take a new product idea that came up from nowhere to become a Unicorn (The start-ups otherwise called Billion Dollar babies – which have the high potential to become a huge success in the coming years)

This is how Bharat Matrimony came into being. While working in New Jersey as a programmer, Murugavel Janakiraman was sending out daily sheets of the traditional calendar details to his friends circle as a community message. In the website there was a small section for matrimony too – a steady traffic to this site was the birth of the bharatmatrimony.com which has entered the Limca Book of Records for the highest number of marriages being facilitated through any website in India. From the traditional methodology of fixing an alliance by letting know in the closed circle of relatives and friends that there is a groom or a bride for whom alliances are being sought out, the scene changed to grooms and brides spread far and wide who now wants to choose the life partner according to their own choices. There was a necessity which was filled in by providing a platform for the grooms and brides to list themselves out.

So the answer to the question of what Bharat Matrimony's problem statement is:

"I want to find a groom/bride from my preferred location and I have to match up the person with my family's choices, and want to look beyond my known circles. What medium can be used to reach out to find a suitable match to my profile?"

Hey you, the next Marc Zuckerberg! I hear you asking the question, "But my product is not based on problems. How do I write this session?" It is in here that you need to narrate the experience that is missing.

If you look at the time before Facebook, the experience of connecting with friends was through personal emails, groups, etc. But now, it is one too many at the same time. So in these kinds of innovative products/services idea, the experience of using the products/services should be written rather than the problem that it is going to solve.

The first climbers to summit Everest without bottled oxygen were Italian Reinhold Messner with Peter Habler in 1978.

The Solution That Is on Offer

Finally, we come to the introduction of the **HERO.**

This section has to provide the following

a. Does this solve a real need/challenge in the current scenario?

B. As a new, innovative product idea, will it give an enhanced experience to the customer or provide a new and easy way of doing things?

So let's accord more attention to the *Hero of Dreams*. Here, you have to talk in full length about your product – it may be a service, it may be a solution, it may be a mechanical device – whatever it may be. It needs all the attention you can give it. Make this the central piece of your storyboard because this needs to be build, this needs to be sold again and again, and all your success, your investors, your partners, your employees and your clients' satisfaction rests on how well this is built/done/explained. I always believe that a brilliant idea alone will not succeed – unless and otherwise it solves or enhances the customers' experience – otherwise that idea belongs more in the trash.

Let's take the event management industry. See the following write-up that is given in the website of an Event Management Company – Subamangala Event Management Company based out of Chennai and catering to all types of weddings and other events as a total package.

Wedding Organizers Chennai

A big paunchy South Indian wedding can be a moment of honour to host and a privilege to attend, but never an easy activity to arrange. Except, you have a company of extraordinarily dedicated and proficient people to be responsible for the accountabilities.

Be it an idea-based wedding, or a common occasion of marriage, we are the planners of an active ritual where everything is particular and suitable. We assure a flowery wedding ceremony to all our esteemed customers who stop by to seek our all-inclusive matrimonial services. Subhamangala is a counsellor as well as a service provider for social ceremonies like housewarming, birthday parties, bridal shower, baby shower, corporate meetings, school fests, college events and others. We conduct the whole affair smoothly, sparing you the worries of corresponding with vendors and suppliers.

See how they list the kind of services they provide as an event management company.

Given below is a precise and sequential blueprint of how we normally execute the complicated process of organizing an event like a wedding.

- *Planning a marriage budget.*
- *Choosing a theme for the wedding.*
- *Booking a suitable venue.*
- *Shopping for the logistical items for the wedding.*
- *Listing the guests for the wedding and the reception.*
- *Picking or designing invitation cards.*
- *Sending them out to the invitees.*
- *Selecting the catering service food menu for the wedding.*
- *Designing custom-made bridal sari.*
- *The Groom's collection for the wedding reception.*
- *Selection of the colour theme for wedding.*
- *Selecting musician, orchestra for the reception.*
- *Conducting the pre-marital rituals.*
- *Nadaswaram melam.*
- *Booking the florist, music band, make-up artist, officiates, etc.*
- *Stage decoration for wedding.*
- *Decorating the banquet halls and the adjoining grounds.*
- *Doing the lighting.*
- *Bridal make-up and dress-up.*
- *Welcoming the guests.*
- *Photography and videography for events.*
- *Accommodation for the guests in star and budget hotels.*
- *Transportation.*
- *Following up with the suppliers.*

- *Personally attending to the bride and groom.*
- *Getting the best honeymoon deals for the preferred destinations.*

Then they go on to state their **Differentiation or USP** (Unique Selling Proposition) as well as the number of events that they have done to establish their credibility or acceptability in the marketplace.

Though wedding concierge service is offered by a multitude of event organizer companies in the market today, you may wonder why you should choose us. Well, that is not because we are big, but because we can make it big for you. We believe that a wedding has significance of more than just a celebration in the lives of a marrying couple and their close ones. So, knowing that, we plug in full effort to make it large and perfect in every possible so that the event is remembered as a gala affair for a very long time. We provide you with many choices because we offer:

- *Wedding assistance all through.*
- *Friendly workers and hardworking professionals to render the service.*
- *Efficient logistic management.*
- *Zero involvement of the clients.*
- *Affordable packages.*
- *Services available at all times of the year.*
- *Services offered for all other social and public ceremonies and gatherings.*

So, dial us now and have the assurance of a peaceful, well-managed D-day.

"Subhamangala as a wedding planner works closely with you and your family to weave a perfect dream. Whether you wish for a small and intimate affair, a large-scale royal production or an exotic destination wedding, we will make

your event special and memorable. Weddings planned by Subhamangala make use of the best of the vendors from across the globe who are best in quality, highly reliable and experimental when it comes to production. Wedding planning at Subhamangala is all about weaving a perfect dream."

Subhamangala *is promoted by Mr. A R Balasubramanian, who has been in the Wedding and Event Management Industry for the past ten years.*

See how they are able to clearly explain Why somebody should buy their services.

As people spend lots of money on weddings and parties, they have to involve themselves in each and every affair in such a way that at the end of the day they feel that they have not seen the wedding of their only son/daughter or that they have not been able to enjoy the functions. That's why a wedding planner-coordinator is required to make you, your family and friends comfortable on the day of the wedding/event.

We, as wedding planners, are here to take care of everything right from invitation cards to honeymoon destinations, theme based weddings, musical extravaganzas and formal parties. We make you comfortable to enjoy each and every function along with your family, friends and relatives. We organize for your comfort.

We have our own designer invitation cards showroom and we also provide destination marriage services. Our caterers prepare their food in their own modern kitchen and serve hygienic food at the wedding place.

I would strongly advice to you spend more pages here about your 'golden baby' and how it is the most beautiful, healthy and strong, and how such an angel baby is needed by the customers from their own perspective rather than from the product perspective. If you see the above write-up about

Subamangala, you would see that it is oriented towards what the user wants rather than just what they offer.

This is the key – Customer Focus and what your product/idea/service would be to the customer

Mt. Everest Facts: 1980 – First solo ascent, by Reinhold Messner and 1988 – First descent by paraglider, by Jean-Marc Boivin

The Market Place and the Product Positioning

Now from the fun stuff, we start moving to serious steps. This is place where our product will be pitted against the whole wicked world. This section will be providing the answers to questions like

1. Does the opportunity so identified by you earlier create enough customer base?
2. Where will the product be sold?
3. What is the market for the product?
4. What is the size of the market?
5. Will it enable the company to grow into the market?
6. At what pace can the market share be gained?

To simply put it, to get a hang on what to write, my advice is that you start taking art classes! I mean, you start drawing the particular person who will be using your product/service/offering. For e.g., if I am making a thermal wear and let us say it is going to be underpants for men, then I would start writing that

- for those in the regions when the temperature comes to lower than say 10 degrees Celsius
- for those males between the ages of 16 and above
- for those males who require the sizes of S, M, L, XL, XXL, XXXL

These are the people who would be buying my product.

So you need to be very specific about the customer and the more specifics you can write, it would be easier for you to write the next few action items that easily and make sure that your marketing campaign succeeds. To refine further, you also need to mention the geography too – is this meant for Indian market or the global market. If it is for the global market, then which are the countries you want to start with?

From this you can derive the total population of that particular region. If it is for the Indian market, then you will take the combined population of the Himalayan region and the neighbouring region.

- The population of India
- The population of the Himalayan region where the temperature can get below 10 degree Celsius
- The percentile of men
- The demographic division age wise

This will give the approximation of the market size. From this, derive the market size for each state too, which will help you to fine tune your marketing and sales strategy.

With regard to the product positioning – where will your product, the thermal wear, fit in here. What is so different about it that you can position this as the best alternate to fighting the cold? I am deliberately not talking about the other products versus your product as we are going to do this little later.

You can draw out a SWOT analysis (Strength, Weakness, Opportunities and Threat) in here and highlight how the strengths and opportunities are the basis for your business growth.

Mt. Everest Facts: 1980 – First winter ascent, by Leszek Cichy and Krzysztof Wielicki and 2000 first descent by ski by Davo Karničar

Competitor Analysis

Here comes the devil wearing the veil. This section is all about

1. The competitors.

2. Our product against the competitors – how will we be able to pit our product against theirs?

3. Our strengths and weakness versus that of our competitors.

4. How can we win against the competition?

5. What would be their reaction to us in terms of their strategy correction - if we aim to blast the market quickly and gain a rapid market share?

You need to do a lot of market research (or you can get somebody to do it for you too) to find out the competitors in the market.

a. What is their product,

b. What are its features,

c. Its pricing,

d. Its market share and

e. What are the marketing efforts that they put in for selling their product?

In a war, it is imperative to understand your enemy before you can start planning your strategy. The same is the case in business too. First, thoroughly understand the competition, if any. If not, understand what is the substitute that is available in the market which your product is going to replace and build all your campaign around this info.

Before answering the first set of questions, It's time for you to play the devil's advocate. I know it is very tough, but you now need to run down your product – My baby is the cutest baby on earth and so how could I find out how that would compare with the child next door. Okay let's start with their age first.

Sl. No.	My baby	My neighbour's baby
1	365 days old	400 days old
2	5kgs weight	6 kgs weight
3	Curly hair	Very thin hair
4	Always happy	Always happy
5	Smiles at everyone	Only smiles at the mother
6	Very friendly	Totally unfriendly
7	Often sick	Very healthy

So out of seven points, my baby fairs well by five points and so **my baby is the best.**

The neighbour, when they do the same analysis their thought process would be – though *my baby is not very friendly, being the healthy baby, my baby is the best.*

Of course, while you need to compare your product like the above, it is not so simple, but still you can start out with the same kind of analogy and go forward for each and every feature that you are talking about. This kind of comparison is highly helpful for you as you will know what kind of improvement your product would need in the later stages or what needs to be highly talked about in your product.

I have copied a sample printer comparison from the internet and see how this is so similar to the baby comparison of the imaginary world.

When you are doing your product comparison with your competitors' product, - you need to be brutally honest and list down the entire features list and how they compare against one another. This will be your blue print for further improvements for your products. But when you are putting this down in the business plan – you need to put all the favourable features of your products with just one or two unfavourable ones to make a great impression about your product. Also, this will be the part that would be analysed by the investor in great detail as it would show how your product would be able to take on the competition in the marketplace.

Having done the comparative analysis, now do a chart which will basically showcase how you can get the customers to buy your product, and by its value, make them swear by it always.

S l. No.	Printer	Model	Colour	Fist copy out time CTO	Black print speed ppm	Input	MRP	Popularity
1	Samsung	ML-2161	Monochrome	8.5sec	20	150	5799	6.5
2	Samsung	ML-1676P	Monochrome	8.5sec	16	150	6899	3.5
3	Canon	C L A S S LBP6680x	Monochrome	7 sec	33	250	43995	5
4	Samsung	CLP-680ND	Colour	17 sec	24	250	39999	5.5
5	Samsung	CLP-365W	Colour		18	150-	17299	4.5
6	Canon	L A S E R S H O T LBP6200d	Monochrome		25	250	12995	8.5
7	LG	PD233	Wireless mobile printer				14990	4.5

Source: http://compareindia.news18.com/products/printers-laser/58

Note of Caution:

INNOVATIVE PRODUCTS/IDEAS:

I can hear your question, "But my product is a new innovation. How do I do the competitor analysis?" You are right. If your product is the first of its genre then what you need to do is a comparison with the existing systems and find out what their negatives are and how your product will overcome those. Take the case of Uber. When it started it was a novel idea, so it had to write up how this would get you a vehicle, that too a top class vehicle at your door step, with a chauffeur who will drop you off at your destination at a lower price than a taxi. It is a different kind of an experience since it involves the owners of the cars who would drive around of their vehicles, which will earn them some additional income as well as put their cars on the roads. This appealed to both the owners as well as the customers and that is how Uber was born. Ola, which came after, could do the comparison with Uber.

So you compare against the existing system and bring out the best of your innovation.

953 people, mostly Sherpa, have summited multiple times totalling 3,861 times (included in the 7,001 total summits).

The Team

The most easily written part of the entire business plan is this section as you need to talk about the founders. Wait, it is not a profile that needs to be given here, but the best of what this person's profile that will make the product to succeed. What needs to be highlighted is that only a great team can deliver great results. In here, the questions that should be answered are

a.   Who are the persons behind this venture?

b.   What do they know about creating a venture, developing a product, delivering the product and earning profit out of the venture.

I can hear the question, "But my qualification and my experience is so different from the product that I have conceived and how will my team come out in this section and appeal to the investors, customers and other founders/employees?" Am I right?

Of course. Then it would be how you came into the product idea and how you are passionate about it and how you would be living, breathing, eating, sleeping with this product is what that needs to be highlighted apart from your professional qualification and experience. Remember these examples when you think about the mismatch of your profile/qualifications with your product.

Mohandas Karamchand Gandhi became Mahatma Gandhi not because of his professional qualification of a degree in law or his practice as barrister – but because of his passion for getting the freedom for the people of his country from the outsiders who were ruling from a distance.

Many a time, the founder becomes famous after the product becomes famous – e.g. Larry Page or Marc Zuckerberg.

This section is meant for the investors and the future employees. This will also be needed when you want to attract co-founders because their experience, qualification, their determination and passion is the precursor for the Successful Product which may be in the conceptualization stage or early stage when we talk about the start-ups.

In the Indian scenario it is not uncommon to notice that you might have started your company in the name of your mother, father or any other relative, and if that is the case, what one do when they would be the directors in the company. If their qualifications and experience are good, then list them down as directors, but if they are there as directors for sentimental purpose, then you can list yourself and your team as the people managing the operations. With investors, however, please disclose the ownership structure and how you and the non-executive persons fit into the company, spelling out the role of each and every director.

Advisors/mentors – You need to mention advisors and mentors, if you are consulting with anybody, as this would also add value to the project. However, with the investors, you need to disclose the financial tie up – whether the advisors have any stake in the company.

1988 – First "cross-over" climb by Chinese, Japanese and Nepalese teams which ascended the peak simultaneously from both the North and South sides of the mountain and descended down the other side.

Marketing Strategy

This is the brain of the baby. The better developed this is, more assured would be the success of your venture. This is as much a blue print for others as it is for you. Here is where you should apply all kinds of marketing principles like 3Cs, 4PS, Porters 5 Forces Model, 7PS extended Marketing Mix etc.- whichever is suitable to you.

This section pertains to the following information

a.   How do you match up your product with your customer requirement, need or expectation?

b.   How do you announce the product to the customer and channel partners?

c.   How will you create the demand for your product?

d.   How will you match the expectation of your product and its pricing?

e. How will you sell it to the customer?

All said and done, this chapter is all about the following questions

"How are you going to announce your product to your customer and make them want to buy it? What is the go-to market (GTM) strategy?"

Hi, this is Professor Sarada Ramani

I am going to take a class on Marketing deviating a little from just talking about the business plan writing as it is essential to understand the concepts before we get into the writing mode. More than anything, instead of cut and paste from the internet, the relevant portions for your type of products, if you can understand the nuances of marketing concepts and then apply it in your product, then you are truly on your way to success.

Let's take the traditional *4 PS – The original marketing concept* propounded by E. Jerome McCarthy in 1960 – Product, Price, Promotion and then Place.

a. **Product**

This can be a tangible or an intangible item which will satisfy a consumer demand – this encompasses all things that are sold under the sun, right from a safety pin to the pages of Facebook where there is a space for providing advertisements.

It is imperative to understand that there is a typical life cycle for each product – start-up, growth phase, maturity phase and then decline phase. Some products S curve, where the product need not necessarily die, but will continue with a steady growth – take pencils for example– there are different varieties, but there is a certain percentage of sales that would come from the writing pencil and this sales will be proportionate to the demographic dividend of the demography.

So be sure to talk about your product life cycle in brief apart from the product development strategies.

b. **Price**

We all know that this is the amount a customer will pay for the product. This is an important aspect of the product as this would determine the profit the company would be getting by selling the product. In today's world, we adopt a lot of pricing strategy to penetrate the market – the freemium, fair pricing, discount pricing, entry pricing etc. Generally speaking the price of the product is **Selling price = Cost + profit**

Of course this holds good for the industrial product. What about the food grains, vegetables, fruits which are dependent on the harvest quantity, demand, cold storage facilities, export market, export regulations, etc. World over these prices are very sensitive and Governments have ensured that the selling price are designed towards the purchasing capability of the masses and that is where the government subsidies, soft loans for the farmers, etc. come in. If you are in this market, please be aware of this tricky situation where the selling price is controlled by the inflation, GDP, etc.

Basic Pricing Strategies

The three basic pricing strategies according to the text books are:

1. *Market skimming pricing* – During the launch of the product the price is kept very high to recover the sunken cost of developing the product. For

example, in TVs and mobile phones, in the high end segment, when a new product is launched, the price is extremely high and it comes down over time. So you might have bought the 45 inch TV when it was launched at a very steep price, but your neighbour, after about 6-8 months, might be buying it at 20% lower cost. This practice is called market skimming pricing strategy. These can be practiced when there is a brand value and unique product value associated with the product.

2. ***Market Penetration Pricing:*** is the one in which a company wants to enter a market or gain a great market share, and so gives a deep discount on their pricing to attract customers to buy the product. The best example is Amazon. When they started selling books online with a minimum of 30% less than actual bookstores that's where the competition ended and Amazon grew and grew to selling from books to all things under the sun.

3. ***Neutral pricing:*** This is the general default strategy of pricing which doesn't look at the price as a tool to gain the marketshare. It is not the strategy where you look at the competitor and fix the pricing, but the pricing is done based on your product

    a. taking the benchmark of what your product offers

    b. the value it has

    c. the advantage position of the product

The best example is vakilsearch.com which is a one stop shop for all the needs of a start-up with regard to starting a company and all the attendant legal and government obligations that needs to be fulfilled like registering a company, creating a Memorandum of Association or Articles of Association as required by the

Ministry of Corporate Affairs. They have a pricing for each service that would be required by the entrepreneur.

Let's now talk of the new normal of the pricing strategies that have come into vogue:

1. **Freemium pricing:** This model is more followed in the digital world where a product or services is provided free of charge, but money/premium is charged for extra usage or for more enhanced features, etc. For example, many of the marketing tools company offer CRM for free for one user or three users in the organization – but will start charging if the number increases. This is based on the fact that the customer acquisition is done at the cost of the base product and the customers start using the product and enjoying all the benefits. So when the customer grows their business they will be upgrade to the premium and paying version. The benefit from this model is that you tend to get a large customer base which can be used for branding, providing customer experience to acquire more customers, marketing and sales promotion, funding, cross selling, etc.

2. **Subscription pricing:** As the name indicates you pay a subscription on a time-based method to avail the services. The earliest to adapt this method of pricing was newspapers and magazines and clubs. This is also followed by many mobile operators, internet providers, software products and websites, business solutions like office cleaning and outdoor cleaning, etc. In effect, those products that are regularly consumed can be priced on this model where the total cost of ownership is very much reduced for the customer.

3. **Pay Per Use:** This is also one the older model which has been given a new usage by the digital world. Our traditional telephone bills – the post-paid, the hotel room rates, etc, are all those that fall under this category of pricing which is based on usage. Pay per click etc. are based on the usage terms.

Note that the pricing strategy has the greatest impact on your marketing strategy as this will affect the demand and the sales of the product. Make sure that you think through your product and its value as that will be perceived by the user, your competition, the demography you play in, the purchasing power of the customers, before you decide the price. It can never be a random choice as too low a price will affect your bottom line and too high a price will make it out of the hands of the customers and both cases are disastrous for the business.

The best example of how the innovative pricing strategy helped an entire industry to gain phenomenal user base is given by the Telecom operators in India. While in the Western world, the growth of the mobile phone was happening in a slow pace, in India the story is that every day there are more than 10,000 new users getting added to the mobile phone bandwagon. All this happened because of the much-thought-out pricing strategy by the mobile operators. In Western countries the operators charge for both the incoming and outgoing calls, whereas in India, while the same pattern was followed initially, they changed to the model of charging the caller only and not the receiver. It enabled the consumer to take the calls from the corporates as well as from their friends and relatives without the fear of having to pay to receive calls. This has enabled the mobile adoption to be extremely faster.

One more point to note about the pricing strategy is that the prices vary depending on the geography of the consumers. For example, India is a highly price sensitive market. People give a lot of thought to 'value for money'. Of course, brand based purchases are there, but the critical mass happens with a sensitive pricing. Here, the profits are made by volume rather than heavy margins. In the Western world, It is more driven by high quality and good service and a lot of brand power. So take all these into consideration when doing the pricing of your product.

c. **Promotion**

We now come to the crux of this chapter. Promotion is the marketing of your product to your chosen audience. While doing that, you need to answer the question - how does the customer know that your product is available for use and how do they find the need to purchase it?

Take nature for example. It is a great example of how marketing strategy has to be different for different things. Nature does the marketing for each of the species in such a wonderful manner. Let's see it in action here. For pollination flowers need bees. If the flower blossoms in the evening, then there is a lovely and heady fragrance as well as the white colour which stands out in the dark. These are the necessary characteristics given to these flowers to announce their presence. For those that bloom in the morning, they are bestowed with colours of various hues and subtle fragrance. So night and day, the flowers, by their fragrance and colours, attract the bees which are in search of the nectar that is found in flowers. Once the bees smell the fragrance in the air or see the bright colours, they know that they have found food and go and settle in the flowers which uses this method to propagate the pollens from one flower to another, and lo and behold, the progeny of the flowers are ensured.

How can we replicate this in our action? As humans, we who can read, speak and listen have to ensure that all the sensory actions are put to use to propagate the news about our product.

Promotion consists of **advertising, public relations, digital marketing and sales promotion.** While the first three are brand building efforts, the last one is the actual sales process.

Advertising encompasses all the communication that is paid for in kind or cash or good will, and will include commercials, internet advertising, print media, billboards, etc. You need to think about the strategy that you are going to adopt in terms of its reach, implication as well as the cost.

PR (Personal Relations) is where you are able to get into the public space by getting written about either in the press or in the internet world by others reviewing your product or participating in fairs and other trade related events, sponsorships, etc. Each and every activity is aimed at increasing your brand/product awareness in the target media.

Digital Marketing: In today's world of the all-encompassing internet, the various strategies you need to adopt to reach out to the netizens of the world needs to be outlined here. Your blogs, your tweets, your LinkedIn and FB posts should all be well thought out to create the best impressions about the brand/product. You also need to concentrate on the information that flows into the net from various sources about your product, your service, etc especially from the customers who discuss the product provide reviews and ratings and testimonials. While such word-of-mouth publicity is the best one, at the same time, anything negative will be the downfall of your business. So in these times, your strategy should also talk about the web based info and the redressal mechanism for any bad comments that may arise.

d. **Place**

Refers to those places from where the product can be bought. It includes not only the physical stores or retail outlet if your product is going to be sold in brick and mortar environment, but also the distribution channels, the franchising arrangements, the virtual world store like the website, FB page, other tele-caller facility, etc needs to be discussed in detail here. If you are selling online, how and where you are selling, what is the guarantee that you would provide that the product will reach the customer when you have received the payment in advance, what is your refund policy, what is the replacement policy, etc have to be addressed here. In India, it was the brilliance of the founders of the home-grown brand **Flipkart** who came up with the idea of **Cash on Delivery,** which means that you can get your products delivered and then pay it to the courier company. This greatly inspired and instilled the confidence in the ecommerce industry itself.

Having talked in great detail about the 4 Ps, in today's world of virtual products like computer-based applications, services, etc, beyond these 4 Ps there are a few more Ps that needs to be addressed as part of the marketing plan.

e. Physical Evidence

When it is service or a virtual product, this becomes important in terms of getting the customers to talk about how the service / product has provided them value and solved the specific problem that has given rise to this product. In case you are in an ideation stage and looking for funding, it would greatly enhance your chances of getting funding if you can create a MVP(Minimum Viable Product) and have customers signed up for the MVP to prove the saleability of your product. MVP means that there is a basic version of the product available for the customers to use and feel the essence of the product. In all other cases, the customers' testimonials are the most important aspect that needs to be presented in here.

People and Process

This topic will be covered in our relevant sections later on.

In conclusion, your marketing plan should be able to demonstrate or give answers to the following questions, especially to the investors as they look at how realistic your strategy is and how effective your pricing will be in the market.

1. How do you reach you customer?

2. How do you promote the intrinsic value of the product?

3. What are the methods that you adopt to reach the message about your product to your customer?

4. Is it an effective pricing strategy that you have followed?

5. How and when will the sales happen the first time, the next time and all the time in a continual manner?

Please note:

This session needs to be done in both an elaborate manner as well as a concise manner, and will be about only the generalities of how the customer will be able to know and buy the product. The first one is essential for both the investment community as well as when you are looking for top level co-founders, but for the rest, make sure only the concise write-up is shown as this is the blueprint of your success and should be treated as confidential document.

The first climbers to summit Everest without bottled oxygen were Italian Reinhold Messner with Peter Habler in 1978. In 2001 – first ascent by a blind climber, Erik Weihenmayer

Sales Strategy

Here we come to action – the movie is produced, and now, to reach this out to the theatres and make sure the audiences are coming to make this a big box office hit is all part of the sales strategy. The required branding would have been done by the marketing team. If you are the only one doing all the work, then remove the hat of the marketer and wear the hat of the salesperson.

You need to demonstrate

a. What your short term sales target and long term sales target are?

b. How you will get into the identified market and target customers?

c. How you will demonstrate the value proposition of the product to the satisfaction of the prospective customer.

d.   How you will finish the deal?

e.   How you will get the invoice paid?

An organization or a product need not be a great product. If it can be sold successfully, then it becomes a great product or a great organization. Whatever is your core expertise – you may be a developer, dreamer, conceptualizer – make yourself into a salesperson first and foremost. It is imperative that you make sure you succeed. Facebook is a fantastic product, but the concept had to be sold to make it all-pervasive. Please watch as many videos of the founders of the great companies. While they will be talking passionately about their product, they would also be consciously or unconsciously be selling their product. UNDERSTAND that in your company, right from the security person to the CEO everyone should be a salesperson. I cannot stress the importance of sales as only sales organizations become successful rather than great or innovative ideas.

Before we start off with the strategy, please take a moment to define the long term and short term sales growth that you are aiming at. These numbers will be the base that will lead to the next chapter or the next task of doing the financial plan.

The sales strategy should address the flow from the lead generation to the sales closure, and about the steps that need to be taken. While the demand generation will be done in the marketing or branding efforts, the sales process is mapped here.

Let's take the example of *skcript* – one of my mentee companies. They have an excellent software product for the large enterprise customers, called Shrink. This product is meant for companies which have a lot of data volume that needs to be stored and retrieved later for their use.

Let's hear what the founders Karthik Kamalakannan and Swathi Kakarla have to say about their product.

SHRINK is the best compression server to reduce your storage landscape. With the most powerful operating system, state-of-the-art machine learning algorithms and an unprecedented technology, SHRINK helps businesses reduce their storage footprint and reuse their existing storage arrays again.

So if they have to list out who their ideal customers are: those entities that produce large data, for e.g. hospitals, architect firms, large IT-BPO companies (which need to store the call records of their clients for a specific period of time), media house, etc. Take the media houses - they have to store each and every movie they have acquired over a period of time and they also have to retrieve them quickly as and when the need arises. So this software helps in not just storage, but helps in compressing the data and storing it. It means if you need 100GB to store some info, you might need just 40-60% of the space to store the same data by using this storage cum compression software.

Let's see how these people have to work out their sales plan. Let's say their short term goal is to have, say three architect firms as their customers, they first need to understand the typical sales cycle for closure. Since they are dealing with large companies, the sales closure may be anything from three to nine months even and let's assume an average of six months. Given this, understand that even if they start from today to close the first sale, it is going to take them an average of six months.

Remember when we talked about customer profiling? Now, they have to understand which geography they should start with or if they should target the entire globe. Of course this strategy will depend on the sales team. This is the second part that will get featured in this topic and let's see it in detail later.

So start with the geography and using the market sizing that has already been done, do the following –

- Start writing about how you are going to target your entire marketing strategy to this segment.
- From the leads, how many prospects you will be able to generate.
- How, from your location, you will be showing the Product demo?
- What is the kind of demo software you will be installing?
- How you will make the customer understand and appreciate the value?
- After the demo period or free usage period, how will you make the customer sign the agreement and start the payment process?
- After the payment, how will you guide the customer in terms of smooth and effective usage of the software?
- How will you trouble shoot the problems, if any?
- Finally, getting the customer testimonials.

This script is not just for the business plan, but for your sales team too. You need to understand that this will become the standard operating procedure for the entire team including the sales, marketing and operation teams, and will make everyone work seamlessly.

Sales Team

This is the sales team you have or would like to have for the execution of your goals. Please note that if you are a start-up, then first talk about the short term goal rather than the long term goal, which can be outlined little later, as our imperative is to first acquire customers to showcase our product and its capabilities. This is the first milestone we need to work for and for this, you should become THE main person who will be the head of sales as it is your product and your passion and who is better qualified than you to talk about its virtues and then close the sale. So remember to talk about a small team which will assist you.

If you are already having a few customers and now want to expand, then it is imperative that you talk about the existing sales team, about where the gap is and how you are going to fulfil the gap.

One note of caution – You can say you want to have a hundred-member sales team even, but the in next chapter, it is going to be financial plan and you need to validate how you can sustain the large team that you talk about and start earning profits ASAP.

One advice I have for the start-ups is that if you are technologist, please choose a co-founder who will be able to do sales and marketing well. This way both of you will be complimenting one another's strength. Remember it is A MUST TO HAVE A SALES AND MARKETING PERSON AS PART OF THE TEAM for your company to succeed.

The youngest person to summit was American Jordan Romero, age 13, on May 23, 2010 from the north side. The oldest person to summit was Japanese Miura Yiuchiro, age 80 on May 23, 2013

Operations Plan

This is the heart of the operation. This also can be split into two parts

    a.   Product Development Plan

    b.   Sales and Distribution Plan

Both needs to be elaborately put for the detailed business plan blueprint. From this detailed plan, you can slice and dice and have a small operational plan for showing to others. In case of co-founder requirement or investor requirement you can take a call on showing the detailed version.

a.   Product Development Plan

This has to be done in detail about how you are going to develop the product, what are the milestones that you have and what is required to reach the milestones. Some of the questions that needs to be answered in here are –

- Does the organization have the ability to produce the product?

- Does it have the right sourcing, collaborating and selling partners?

- In case of the physical product, has the organization chosen a location to produce or distribute the products without any legal or environmental issues or other issues like the easy availability of power, communication, easy access, workforce, etc.

If it is a physical product, then before setting up a huge manufacturing facility, you may probably be doing a few sample pieces. With if that is the case, then you need to write how you are going to do the sample piece, whether by outsourcing or getting it done in a lab or whatever methodology you are going to adapt. You need to clearly spell out how fast you can build up your inventory as and when the demand for the product picks up, since you cannot have a situation where you have customers waiting to buy the product, but the availability of the product is in question. This will deeply affect your credibility and your ability to deliver. So be sure to have all these in place. In total, you need to draw the map with the suppliers, vendors, manufacturers, quality assurance teams, etc to give the full picture of how the product will be developed. You need to demonstrate that at every stage of the input and output, the QC/QA will be well taken care of to bring out the best product to the market.

In case it is a technology-related product, you need to spell out the technology in detail and how you are taking care of future prospects, since technology tend to change faster. As in the case of the physical product, you also need to demonstrate how you can bring out the product based on its milestones, what kind of hardware, software and people requirements you have and how you will be able to fulfil them. It is also the right place for you to talk about the backups plans of the product and the security systems that are in place for protecting the data/the code, etc.

b. **Sales and Distribution Plan**

Whether it is a physical product or a digital product, this section talks about

- How you will create and maintain your customer data or CRM.
- What will happen when the invoice is raised for the purchase of the product?
- What the licensing requirements are.
- How your distributors, channel partners, if any, will sell this product to the end customer.
- What the after-sales service arrangements are.
- About replacements and returns, etc.

1998 – Fastest to reach the summit via the southeast ridge (South Col), without supplemental oxygen, by Kazi Sherpa, in 20 hours and 24 minutes. 2004 – Fastest to reach the summit via the southeast ridge (South Col), with supplemental oxygen, by Pemba Dorje, in 8 hours and 10 minutes

Financial Plans

I will compare the financial plan to be the respiratory system of the entire operation. Remember that No money is equivalent to No oxygen and that the body can withstand only a few minutes without oxygen. Same is the case with any business also, whether it is for profit or otherwise. Here, the sales number, the pricing of the product, the size of the team, all have larger implication to what you spend and what you earn.

It is very simple. You invest money for buying the necessary equipment, pay the various operational costs like team salary, electricity bills, communication cost, marketing cost, sales expenditure etc. In return you get the revenue from the sales of your product or service, as and when it happens.

The balance sheet or Profit and Loss accounts are all zero sum game that is - if there is 100$ expenditure, then there has to be a corresponding 100$ inflow. How this 100$ comes into the business can be - by your own funds invested into the business, or the loan from the bank, friends, relatives, investor funds or your sales. You don't need to understand all the terminologies yourself, you can take the help of a Chartered Accountant to get this prepared, but you need to give the inputs. You need to go to a Chartered Accountant with your projected numbers or the revenue you expect to get from the sale of your products/service, your expenses, your proposed marketing and selling/distribution costs. With these figures given by you, the Chartered Accountant will help you to prepare the necessary documents. However, once it is prepared, take time to understand each and every line item so that you will know the numbers by heart and you can present it professionally when the need arises.

The financial projections are given as

- Project Plan
- Balance Sheet
- Profit and Loss Account
- Cash flow
- Breakeven analysis

The first three are those that need to be done by professionally qualified people, the last two need to be prepared by you initially and then taken to the CPA or Chartered Accountant to get it vetted and redone.

The cash flow will indicate what your burn rate or the amount you need for a specific period of time – whether monthly/quarterly or annually. For this expenditure, how do you get the money in is what needs to be worked out by you. My advice is that please prepare this cash flow every month and you will know the pulse of your spending and you can control it and do what is necessary and leave out the extras.

The **breakeven analysis** is an important document which will tell you and the investors when you would start earning more money than what you have put in the business. But, understand that the numbers have to be validated by your operational plan, marketing and sales plan and the pricing that you are going to fix for the products. Any investor or banker will look through this section with a fine comb to understand whether it is worthwhile to invest or fund and how much funding needs to be done.

2006 - Lhakpa Sherpa summits for the 6th time, breaking her own record for most successful female Everest climber. 2013 - Melissa Arnot, American, summits for the 5th time breaking her own record for most successful summits by any non-Sherpa woman

Milestones

This is one part which you can have or you don't need to have – but I would strongly suggest that you do write it out too and have it as part of your business plan. Here is a place, where you can define your

    a.   Short term goal

    b.   Long term goal

While the short term goal will help you to get the first foothold, the long term goal would talk about your dream in detail. Your milestones in terms of the following aspects of business should be dealt with - both in short term and long term perspective.

- Product development
- Team formation
- Marketing and branding effects
- Sales achievement

This section will help you to shape your journey very well and also give the investors a clear picture of what you have in mind. So go do it with concentration. I suggest you do it for the first three months, six months, twelve months, two years and five years if possible. Understand that this has to align with your SMART goal for yourself. If both are in sync, the battle is already won.

282 people (169 westerners and 113 Sherpas) have died on the Everest from 1924 to August 2015. Of the deaths, 102 died attempting to summit without using supplemental oxygen. The top cause of death was from a fall, avalanche, exposure and altitude sickness. From 1923 to 1999, 170 people died on the Everest with 1,169 summits or 14.5%. But the deaths drastically declined from 2000 to 2015 with 5,832 summits and 112 deaths or 1.9%. The reduction in deaths is primarily due to better gear, weather forecasting and more people climbing with commercial operations.

Risk – Plan and Mitigation

This is a very important section where utmost concentration needs to be given, as this is like what needs to be done when something goes wrong. Life and business are full of uncertainties. Though we plan thoroughly, still something happens, and hence we always need to have option B and option C. In life you can take things as they come, but in business you need to plan for all eventualities to enable a successful journey as an entrepreneur.

So what kind of risks should we start thinking about?

- Product risk
- Operations risk
- Competition risk
- Financial risk
- Customer risk

- Legal/environmental/risks

When we start our business we don't necessarily start thinking negative about the product, but we need to understand from different perspectives about each one of the above risk and then continue. You need to come up with the mitigation plan for each of these risks too, including risk mitigation plans for a scenario in which the team falls apart, the entire batch of products are all defective when you have a very tight delivery schedule, the government enacting a new law that prohibits the sale of your genre of products, etc.

To make you understand the criticality of this section, let me give you a live example. In a Pitchfest in which I was part of, a young man was so passionate about his product and he had done a lot of market research, market sizing etc,. The product idea was to manufacture a Plastic holder for keeping the mobile phone securely in front of a bike rider so that the rider can easily look into the smart phone. The inherent weakness in this idea is whether the government will allow the riders to have this product as part of their bikes since this will be a great risk for the other road users. Here the users or the customers are not the risk; it is the legality of the product which is at risk as this will be a danger for the other road users. There was no mitigation for this risk and hence the young man had to drop his idea totally.

The above example will make you understand that you can think in terms of various angles about your business idea. The PEST analysis (Political, Economical, Society and Technology) will be highly helpful to validate various risks and opportunities of your product/service. Discuss with your friends, mentors, the team and other professionals to have a deep dive and then fill the relevant sections.

> *There have been 7,001 summits of Everest through August 2015 on all routes by 4,093 different people. 953 people, mostly Sherpa, have summited multiple times, totalling 3,861 times (included in the 7,001 total summits). The Nepal side is more popular with 4,421 summits compared to 2,580 summits from the Tibet side. 193 climbers summited without supplemental oxygen through August 2015, about 2.7%. 14 climbers have traversed from one side to the other.*

Exit Plan

I can hear a voice. We are talking about growing and when should I start thinking about exit. Even if it is your baby, at some point of time you need to let it go like how your parents have let you go in slow phases – first for playschool, then for kindergarten, etc.

The exit plan is an integral part of the business plan since it will not only make you think of you as an expendable part of the growth story of the product, but also give the investors their way to make good their investment in your company. Understand that nobody invests in the company for charity but to make money out of their investment. So this section will spell out how this will happen.

There are **three ways to doing the exit strategy**

1. Management buyout

2. Strategic Acquisitions

3. IPO

1. **Management Buyout**

   Understand that you are the management when you start your company. If you bootstrap or go for debt funding to grow the company, you still continue to own hundred per cent of the shares as well as full management. However, if you go for seed funding, series A, B, etc, then slowly your equity or the percentage of ownership comes down. But remember that in all these efforts the net worth of your company and thereby your individual net worth may be going up. For e.g. instead of a hundred per cent owner of a 10,000$ company, you may be a sixty per cent owner of a 250,000$ company.

   This is a slow process of the management buyout and you decide the dilution of your shares by various milestones that need to be achieved with respect to the growth of the company and the financial need as the case of may be. Sometimes, your sell out of the shares can be part of the monetization efforts too where the amount that comes from the share purchase need not necessarily go towards only the company, but can be to your personal account too.

2. **Strategic Acquisition**

   In Strategic acquisition, for various reasons another company may want to merge their company with yours either by paying cash or giving stocks or both in the acquiring company. The best example is the acquisition of WhatsApp by Facebook for a whooping nineteen billion dollars or the Ola cab-for-hire company acquiring the shares of Taxi for Sure to create a bigger company. The acquirer may or may not retain you or your team. The benefit will be the liquidity that you would have since the acquirer may want to buy the entire shares, but the downside is that you lose your baby totally.

3. **IPO**

   It is making you company public by selling a portion of your shares. You are still there, your baby is with you and you get your liquidity too, but the downside is that you come into the public domain and you are answerable to the all unknown hundreds of shareholders that bind large corporates. Also, there has to be a large size before you can go for the IPO since there is a lot of money as well as the time and effort involved in promoting the share.

All these are keenly read by the investors as it will give them how they can make their investment earn profit for them. This is also of interest to the co-founders or the team.

Babu Chiri Sherpa spent the night on the summit in 1999. Apa Sherpa and Phurba Tashi both hold the record for most summits with 21, the most recent one in 2013. Over 33,000 feet of fixed rope is used each year to set the South Col route. You have to be at least sixteen to climb Everest from the south side and eighteen from the north. Climbers burn over 10,000 calories each day, double that on the summit climb. Climbers will lose 10 to 20 lbs during the expedition.

Sharing the Business Plan

I have chosen to include this chapter in this book for the simple reason that many are not aware about what to share with whom. Either people are very paranoid about even talking a little more in detail about their product, or on the other hand, people so easily share things with whoever asks for the business plan. Through various chapters I have written in detail about what portions needs to be shared with whom.

Before sharing the business plan, please get a Non-Disclosure Agreement signed with the person with whom you are going to share.

Note: Many venture capitalists or funders may or may not like to sign NDA with everyone who is coming to their doorsteps for their funding needs. My advice to you is that do homework on the person whom you are going to meet and get the feel of him/her or the company. You can politely ask, "But if they say no", then take a call based on your intuition about sharing the business plan.

Of course, do detailed business plan for your own self and this should talk about all the outcomes - both the positives and the negatives. This has to be brutally honest. It should consider the best case scenarios as well as the worst case scenarios for every chapter – but keep this locked away and DO NOT SHARE this with anyone.

After this, start creating **different versions of the business plan.**

1. For investors
2. For finding co-founders
3. For getting the right team
4. For laying out the marketing strategy
5. For executing the sales plan
6. For short term goal definition, strategy, planning and action
7. For long term goal definition, strategy, planning and action

Name all these appropriately, and remember, for whatever reason you make corrections in any one of these, ensure that the corrections go back to the parent documents as well as the other versions.

There are eighteen different climbing routes on the Everest. It takes 40 days to climb Mt. Everest in order for the body to adjust to the high altitude. There is 66% less oxygen in each breath on the summit of the Everest than at sea level. Thin nylon ropes are used to keep climbers from falling. Climbers wear spikes on their boots, called crampons, and use ice axes to help stop a fall. Thick, puffy suits filled with goose feathers keep climbers warm. Climbers start using bottled oxygen at 26,000 feet but it only makes a 3,000 foot difference in how they feel so at 27,000 feet, they feel like they are at 24,000 feet.

Conclusion

There are successful organizations and not-so-successful organizations. Of course, not everyone started with a business plan in the format that has been described above, but in some form or other, would have been there to provide the required guidelines, forecast, strategy, etc. Throughout the book, I have dealt with companies or start-ups which are just blossoming out, while in the first chapter, I talked about even corporates that go for business plan.

Every corporate has its own business plan, which comes from either a top down approach that says, "This is the business we want to do for this product," and from there it is broken down for each region and then the plan is written accordingly. Or it goes from bottom up where each region, either product wise or region wise, come up with their business plan and all collated become the business plan of the company, with necessary course corrections done by the top management. But believe me, there is a blueprint for all the divisions and this is the basis on which all corporates work on to ensure that their market share is won, gained, protected, etc.

I have made it sound it easy, but I know it is difficult. I started writing out the business plan for this book and I am struggling in some places as there are a lot of unknowns, but I am walking the talk and will be creating the blueprint for myself.

Remember, your success depends on all your actions and if your business plan is going to ensure that business – start writing it down right away. I am wishing you all success in your business ventures.

I would be happy to help you out as and when you require. Please feel free to connect with me.

Bibliography

1. http://www.alanarnette.com/kids/everestfacts.php regarding the facts about Mount Everest.

2. https://en.wikipedia.org/wiki/Mount_Everest

3. www.bharatmatrimony.com

4. http://subhamangala.com/decorators.html

5. www.skricpt.com

6. www.vakilsearch.com

www.ingramcontent.com/pod-product-compliance
Lightning Source LLC
Chambersburg PA
CBHW051329220526
45468CB00004B/1558